Science
DICTIONARY

David Glover

a
b
c
d
e
f
g
h
i
j
k
l
m
n
o
p
q
r
s
t
u
v
w
x
y
z

adult

a fully grown animal or plant

amphibian

an animal that lives some of the time on land but lays its eggs in water

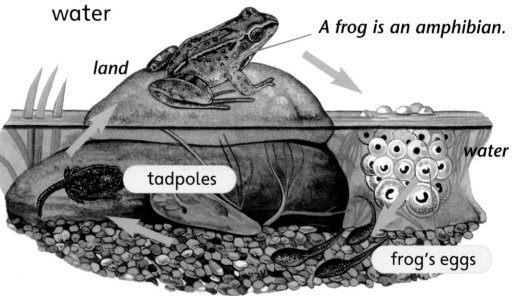

A frog is an amphibian.

land

water

tadpoles

frog's eggs

animal

a living thing that breathes and moves about

arm

the part of a person's body between the shoulder and the hand
➤ *See also:* hand

arm

baby

a newly born or very young animal

battery

a small container that makes and stores electricity
➤ *See also:* electricity

bean

a large seed that grows inside the long pod of a plant
➤ *See also:* pod, seed

bean

blind

unable to see

blossom

small flowers on trees in spring
➤ *See also:* flower

blossom

body

all the parts that make up an animal

to boil

to heat a liquid until it gets very hot and turns into a gas
➤ *See also:* gas, liquid, steam

boiling water

bubble

a ball of gas inside a liquid
➤ *See also:* gas, liquid

bud

a new part of a plant which grows and unfolds into a leaf or a flower

bud

camouflage

the special patterns, shapes and colours on the bodies of some animals that make them hard to see

A chameleon uses camouflage.

carnivore

an animal that eats other animals
➤ *See also:* herbivore

cement

a grey powder that sets like rock when it is mixed with water

chest

the front, top part of the body

chest

colour blind

unable to tell apart certain colours, such as red and green

conductor
a substance that lets electricity, heat or sound pass through it easily
➤ *See also:* electricity

to crawl
to move the body close to the ground

to decay
to rot

dinosaur
a kind of prehistoric animal that died out 65 million years ago
➤ *See also:* prehistoric

dinosaur

ear

a part of the body that helps an animal to hear

Earth

the name of the planet we live on

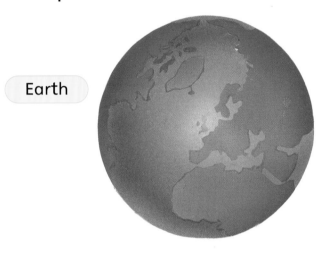

Earth

egg

a round or oval object from which an animal begins to grow

➤ *See also:* nest, yolk

egg

elbow

the joint in the middle of an arm
that is able to bend
➤ *See also:* arm

elbow

electricity

a form of energy used for lighting,
heating and making things work
➤ *See also:* battery

environment

the land, water and air around the
place where an animal or plant lives

environment

eye

a part of the body that helps an
animal to see

finger

one of the five parts on the end
of a hand used for
grasping and gripping
➤ *See also:* hand, thumb

finger

fire

the flame, heat and light that is
produced when something burns

fire

fish

an animal with scales that lives in
water, breathes with gills and
swims with fins
➤ *See also:* gill, swim

flour

a powder made from crushing the
seeds of corn and other plants

flower

the coloured part of a plant from
which seeds or fruit grow
➤ *See also:* fruit, seed

flour

to fly

to move through the air
using wings
➤ *See also:* wing

A bird flies.

food

the substances that animals eat
and plants use to live and grow

foot

the lower end of a leg on which
an animal stands
➤ *See also:* leg

force

something which can make things
move, stop or change direction
➤ *See also:* friction, gravity, pull, push

fossil

the remains of an animal or
plant that are preserved in stone

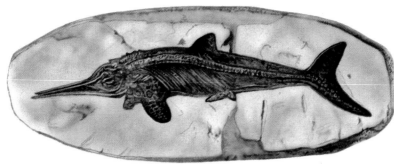

*A fossil of
fish bones*

to freeze

to become solid as a result of cold
➤ *See also:* ice

friction

the force of one thing rubbing over
another thing
➤ *See also:* force

fruit

a part of a plant that
has seeds in it and which
can often be eaten
➤ *See also:* plant, seed

fruit

gas
a very thin, light substance such as the air

gill
the part of an underwater animal that is used for breathing

gill

glass
a hard material that is transparent and easy to break
➤ *See also:* material, transparent

gravity
the force that pulls everything to the Earth
➤ *See also:* force

to grow
to become bigger

A baby grows into an adult.

habitat

the natural home of a plant or an animal

hand

the lower part of an arm that is used for grasping, holding and touching things

➤ *See also:* finger, thumb

to hatch

to break out from an egg

➤ *See also:* egg

A young crocodile hatches from an egg.

head

the part of an animal's body where its eyes, ears, nose, mouth and brain are normally found

herbivore

an animal that only eats plants

➤ *See also:* carnivore

ice

frozen water
➤ *See also:* freeze, water

insect

a small animal with three
main body parts, six legs
and usually a pair of wings

insect

insulator

a material that is difficult for
electricity, heat or sound to
pass through
➤ *See also:* conductor

knee

the joint in the middle of the leg
that is able to bend
➤ *See also:* leg

knee

leaf

the green flat part that grows
from the stem of a plant

leaf

leg

the part of a body between the
hip and the foot that is used for
moving around

light

the brightness that makes it
possible to see things

liquid

a substance that takes up the
shape of the container into
which it is poured
➤ *See also:* water

magnet

a piece of metal that attracts things with iron in them

magnet

marine

to do with the sea

material

the substance from which something is made

to melt

to make something liquid when heated

➤ *See also:* liquid

Chocolate melts when it is heated.

metal

a material that is hard and
sometimes strong
➤ *See also:* material

Moon

a small, natural satellite that
moves around the Earth in space

Moon

nest

a place where some animals lay
their eggs
➤ *See also:* egg

paper

a thin, flat sheet of material
used for writing or painting
➤ *See also:* material

pet

an animal that is kept and
cared for by humans

plant

a living thing that makes its
own food from water,
air and sunlight

plastic

a material that is light
and easy to bend
➤ *See also:* material

*Lots of things are
made from plastic.*

pod

a long case of a plant that
holds seeds
➤ *See also:* bean, seed

predator

an animal that hunts and kills
other animals for food
➤ *See also:* prey

predator

prehistoric

the time before written records
were kept

prey

an animal that is hunted and
killed by a predator for food
➤ *See also:* predator

to pull

to move something towards oneself
➤ *See also:* force

pupil

the black part of an eye that
lets light through
➤ *See also:* eye

pupil

to push

to move something away from
oneself
➤ *See also:* force

- **to recycle**
  to use again, or to make new products from old materials

recycling bins

Glass   Plastic   Aluminium cans

- **reptile**
  a cold-blooded animal with a backbone and scaly skin

- **root**
  the part of a plant that grows down into the soil

- **season**
  one of the four parts of each year

- **seed**
  the part of a plant that grows into a new plant
  ➤ *See also:* plant

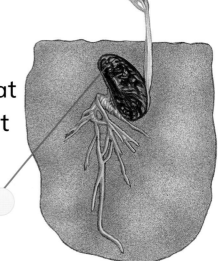

seed

to sense

to be able to see, hear, touch, taste and smell

shoot

the new part of a plant that grows out from a seed
➤ *See also:* bud, seed

stampede

a group of animals running together to get away from danger

Horses stampeding

steam

a gas that is formed when water is boiled
➤ *See also:* boil, gas, water

● **stem**

the main part of a plant that grows up into the air
➤ *See also:* plant

● **sting**

a sharp point of an animal or plant that sometimes contains poison

sting

● **Sun**

the huge bright star that provides heat and light for the Earth
➤ *See also:* Earth

Sun

● **to swim**

to move through water with a gliding motion

thumb
the short, thick digit at the side of
a hand
➤ *See also:* finger, hand

thumb

transparent
able to see through

veterinarian or vet
an animal doctor

volcano
a mountain with an opening where
melted rock and hot gases come up
from under the ground
➤ *See also:* Earth

volcano

water

a transparent liquid found all over the Earth as oceans, rivers, lakes and rain

➤ *See also:* liquid, transparent

water

wing

the part of the body that flying animals use to lift themselves off the ground

➤ *See also:* fly

wood

the strong part of trees that is used to make things

yolk

the yellow part inside an egg which is used to feed the growing animal

➤ *See also:* animal, egg